Machiavelli:
Mastering the Art of Realpolitik

Niccolò Machiavelli was born on May 3, 1469, in Florence, Italy, during the height of the Italian Renaissance. He was the third child of Bernardo Machiavelli, a lawyer from an ancient Tuscan family, and Bartolomea di Stefano Nelli. Though not born into nobility, Machiavelli grew up in a politically tumultuous and intellectually vibrant environment.

As a young boy, Machiavelli received a humanist education, which emphasized the study of classical literature, philosophy, and history. These early influences played a crucial role in shaping his intellectual development and later career. He showed a keen interest in political matters from an early age and demonstrated a sharp intellect.

In 1498, at the age of 29, Machiavelli began his political career when he was appointed as a Second Chancellor to the Republic of Florence. This position gave him the opportunity to engage in diplomacy, serve as a trusted advisor, and participate in various governmental affairs. Florence, at the time, was a thriving city-state known for its flourishing arts, culture, and vibrant political scene.

During his tenure as a diplomat, Machiavelli represented Florence in several important diplomatic missions, including trips to France, Germany, and the Italian city-states. These experiences exposed him to different political systems and allowed him to interact with prominent leaders and thinkers of the time.

In 1502, Machiavelli was sent on a diplomatic mission to the court of Cesare Borgia, the ambitious and ruthless son of Pope Alexander VI. This encounter left a lasting impression on Machiavelli, as he witnessed firsthand the practicalities of power and the Machiavellian tactics employed by Borgia to achieve his goals. The insights gained during this mission would later inform Machiavelli's political theories.

In addition to his diplomatic duties, Machiavelli also served as a military official in the Florentine Republic. He played an active role in the city's defense and took part in various military campaigns. Machiavelli believed that a strong military was essential for the stability and security of a state, and his experiences in the military greatly influenced his later writings on war and strategy.

Throughout his career, Machiavelli became well-known for his shrewdness, pragmatism, and acute observations of human nature. He developed a reputation as a skilled negotiator, capable of understanding the complexities of politics and adapting to changing circumstances.

Unfortunately, Machiavelli's political fortunes took a downturn when the Medici family, who had been exiled from Florence, returned to power in 1512. The Medici saw Machiavelli as a political threat and accused him of conspiracy. Machiavelli was imprisoned, tortured, and subsequently banished from political life.

Exiled and stripped of his previous responsibilities, Machiavelli retreated to his country estate near Florence. It was during this period of forced retirement that he turned his attention to writing and produced his most famous work, "The Prince." Drawing upon his vast experiences in politics and diplomacy, Machiavelli sought to distill the principles of effective leadership and governance in his magnum opus.

Writings, Legacy, and Influence

Following his exile from political life, Niccolò Machiavelli dedicated himself to writing and produced some of his most influential works during this period.

"The Prince" (Il Principe), written in 1513 and published posthumously in 1532, remains Machiavelli's most famous and controversial work. It is a political treatise that explores the nature of power, effective leadership, and the acquisition and maintenance of political control. In "The Prince," Machiavelli offers pragmatic advice to rulers, emphasizing the importance of political stability and practicality over strict adherence to moral or ethical principles. He argues that a ruler should be willing to use any means necessary to preserve power, even if those means are seen as ruthless or deceitful. This pragmatic approach to politics led to the label of "Machiavellian" being associated with cunning and unscrupulous behavior in governance.

Another notable work by Machiavelli is "Discourses on Livy" (Discorsi sopra la prima deca di Tito Livio), written around 1517 and published in 1531. Unlike "The Prince," which focused on princely rule, "Discourses on Livy" examines the dynamics of republican government. Machiavelli draws insights from ancient Roman history, particularly the works of the historian Livy, to analyze the strengths and weaknesses of different political systems. In this work, he advocates for citizen participation, civic virtue, and a strong military as essential elements for the success of a republic.

Machiavelli's writings extended beyond political theory. In "The Art of War" (Dell'arte della guerra), written between 1519 and 1520 (and published in 1521), he delves into military strategy, tactics, and the importance of a well-disciplined army. Drawing from his personal experiences in the military, Machiavelli provides practical advice on warfare, including the organization of armies, the selection of commanders, and the importance of understanding one's enemies.

Despite their significant contributions to political thought, Machiavelli's works were met with both acclaim and criticism. Some praised his realistic and pragmatic approach to politics, considering his writings as valuable guides for rulers navigating the complexities of power. Others condemned him for his seemingly amoral suggestions and perceived endorsement of tyrannical behavior.

His works challenged conventional wisdom, offering a new understanding of politics that emphasized practicality and effectiveness. Machiavelli's focus on the realities of power, the dynamics of leadership, and the relationship between the ruler and the governed influenced later philosophers like Hobbes, John Locke, Jean-Jacques Rousseau etc.

Over time, Machiavelli's name became synonymous with cunning and Machiavellianism. However, it is essential to note that his writings were often intended as reflections on the political realities of his time rather than a prescriptive endorsement of ruthless behavior. Machiavelli aimed to provide practical guidance to rulers in an era of shifting alliances, power struggles, and unstable governments.

Niccolò Machiavelli's legacy extends far beyond his lifetime. His works continue to spark intellectual debate and are studied in political science, philosophy, and history courses worldwide. While opinions about his ideas vary, there is no denying the lasting impact he has had on our understanding of politics, power, and the complexities of governance.

Navigating the Political Landscape: Key Ideas from Machiavelli's Works

Machiavelli's ideas and philosophy emerged from the politically tumultuous Italian Renaissance era, characterized by internal factional conflicts, constant power struggles, and shifting allegiances.

In this turbulent context, his works aimed to provide practical guidance to rulers, emphasizing the realities of power and the imperative of effective leadership. Here are some of the key concepts from his writings:

REALISM AND PRACTICALITY: Machiavelli emphasized the importance of realism and practicality in politics. He believed that rulers should base their decisions on an accurate understanding of human nature and the realities of power, rather than being guided solely by moral or idealistic principles.

CONSIDERATION OF AMORAL POLITICS AND THE PRIMACY OF POWER: Machiavelli's writings often challenge conventional moral principles in politics. He argued that rulers should be willing to set aside traditional ethical norms if necessary to acquire and maintain political power. According to Machiavelli, political success should be measured by the ability to secure and strengthen one's position rather than conforming to moral ideals.

THE ENDS JUSTIFY THE MEANS: Machiavelli famously stated that "the ends justify the means." He believed that rulers should prioritize the preservation of their power and the stability of the state over moral considerations. He also argued that if a goal is morally important, any method of getting it is acceptable. In his view, the justification of an action lies in its ability to produce a desirable outcome, regardless of the methods utilized.

PRAGMATISM AND FLEXIBILITY: Machiavelli stressed the importance of pragmatism and flexibility in political decision-making.

He advocated for rulers to adapt their strategies and tactics to the changing circumstances of politics and to be willing to make calculated adjustments to achieve their goals.

FORTUNA AND VIRTÙ: Machiavelli discussed the concepts of fortuna (fortune or luck) and virtù (virtue or strength). He argued that successful rulers needed to possess both, with virtù representing their individual qualities and capabilities, and fortuna representing external factors beyond their control. Machiavelli emphasized the importance of a ruler's virtù in navigating and overcoming the challenges posed by fortuna.

THE ROLE OF THE STATE: Machiavelli believed that the state should be the central focus of political attention and that the well-being and stability of the state should take precedence over other considerations. He emphasized the importance of a strong state and a capable ruler in maintaining order and protecting the interests of the people.

THE ROLE OF THE CITIZEN: In "Discourses on Livy," Machiavelli discussed the importance of active and engaged citizenship. He argued that a successful republic required the participation and civic virtue of its citizens, including their willingness to defend the state and serve in its military.

While his ideas continue to provoke debate, Niccolò Machiavelli's enduring legacy lies in his ability to provoke critical thinking and shape the discourse on political theory, leaving an indelible mark on the study of governance for centuries to come.

Everyone who wants
to know what will
happen ought to
examine what
has happened:
everything in this
world in any epoch
has their replicas
in antiquity.

Men in general judge
more by the sense of
sight than by the
sense of touch,
because everyone can
see but few can test
by feeling. Everyone
sees what you seem to
be, few know what you
really are; and those
few do not dare take
a stand against the
general opinion.

When you disarm
your subjects,
you offend them by
showing that either
from cowardliness
or lack of faith, you
distrust them; and
either conclusion
will induce them
to hate you.

It ought to be remembered
that there is nothing more
difficult to take in hand,
more perilous to conduct,
or more uncertain in its
success, than to take the lead
in the introduction of a new
order of things. Because the
innovator has for enemies
all those who have done well
under the old conditions,
and lukewarm defenders in
those who may do well under
the new. This coolness arises
partly from fear of the
opponents, who have the laws
on their side, and partly
from the incredulity of men,
who do not readily believe
in new things until they
have had a long experience
of them.

No enterprise is
more likely to
succeed than one
concealed from the
enemy until it is
ripe for execution.

All courses of action
are risky, so prudence
is not in avoiding
danger (it's impossible),
but calculating risk
and acting decisively.
Make mistakes of
ambition and not
mistakes of sloth.
Develop the strength to
do bold things, not the
strength to suffer.

When evening comes, I return
home and go into my study.
On the threshold I strip off
my muddy, sweaty clothes of
everyday, and put on the robes
of court and palace, and in this
graver dress I enter the antique
courts of the ancients and am
welcomed by them, and there
I taste the food that alone is
mine, and for which I was born.
And there I make bold to speak
to them and ask the motives of
their actions, and they, in
their humanity, reply to me.
And for the space of four hours
I forget the world, remember no
vexation, fear poverty no more,
tremble no more at death; I pass
indeed into their world.

Is it better to be loved rather than feared, or feared rather than loved? It might perhaps be answered that we should wish to be both: but since love and fear can hardly exist together, if we must choose between them, it is far safer to be feared than loved because... love is preserved by the link of obligation which, owing to the baseness of men, is broken at every opportunity for their advantage; but fear preserves you by a dread of punishment which never fails.

A multitude is strong
while it holds together,
but so soon as each of
those who compose it
begins to think of his
own private danger,
it becomes weak
and contemptible.

It will always happen
that he who is not your
friend will request
your neutrality
and he who is your
friend will ask you
to declare yourself
by taking up arms.

Nature has so created men
that they are able to desire
everything but are not able
to attain everything:
so that the desire being
always greater than the
acquisition, there results
discontent with the
possession and little
satisfaction to themselves
from it. From this arises the
changes in their fortunes;
for as men desire, some to
have more, some in fear of
losing their acquisition,
there ensues enmity and war,
from which results the ruin
of that province and the
elevation of another.

He who has not first
laid his foundations
may be able with
great ability to lay
them afterwards,
but they will be laid
with trouble to the
architect and danger
to the building.

Present wars
impoverish the
lords that win
as much as those
that lose.

There should be
many judges,
for few will
always do the
will of few.

The best fortress
is to be found in the
love of the people,
for although you may
have fortresses they
will not save you if
you are hated by the
people.

Friendships that are acquired by a price and not by greatness and nobility of character are purchased but are not owned, and at the proper moment they cannot be spent.

Injuries ought to be
done all at one time,
so that, being tasted
less, they offend less;
benefits ought to be
given little by little,
so that the flavour of
them may last longer.

It is a common
failing of man not
to take account of
tempests during
fair weather.

It is truly a marvelous thing to consider to what greatness Athens arrived in the space of one hundred years after she freed herself from the tyranny of Pisistratus... The reason is easy to understand, for it is the common good and not private gain that makes cities great... and however much damage it does to this or that private individual, those who benefit from the said common good are so numerous that they are able to advance in spite of the inclination of the few citizens who are oppressed by it.

There are three kinds
of intelligence: one
kind understands
things for itself, the
other appreciates what
others can understand,
the third understands
neither for itself nor
through others.
This first kind is
excellent, the second
good, and the third
kind useless.

For my part I consider
that it is better to be
adventurous than
cautious, because
fortune is a woman...
and it is seen that she
allows herself to be
mastered by the
adventurous rather
than by those who go to
work more coldly. She
is, therefore, always,
woman-like, a lover of
young men, because they
are less cautious, more
violent, and with more
audacity command her.

A man who is used to
acting in one way
never changes; he
must come to ruin
when the times, in
changing, no longer
are in harmony
with his ways.

It is of the greatest
important in this world
that a man should know
himself, and the measure
of his own strength and
means; and he who knows
that he has not a genius
for fighting must learn
how to govern by the
arts of peace.

Men rise from one
ambition to another:
first, they seek to
secure themselves
against attack, and
then they attack
others.

This return of
Republics back to their
principles also results
from the simple virtue
of one man, without
depending on any law
that excites him to any
execution: none the
less, they are of such
influence and example
that good men desire to
imitate him, and the
wicked are ashamed to
lead a life contrary
to those examples.

The fact is that a
man who wants to act
virtuously in every
way necessarily
comes to grief
among so many who
are not virtuous.

The Romans never allowed a trouble spot to remain simply to avoid going to war over it, because they knew that wars don't just go away, they are only postponed to someone else's advantage. Therefore, they made war with Philip and Antiochus in Greece, in order not to have to fight them in Italy... They never went by that saying which you constantly hear from the wiseacres of our day, that time heals all things. They trusted rather their own character and prudence- knowing perfectly well that time contains the seeds of all things, good as well as bad.

The vulgar crowd
always is taken by
appearances, and
the world consists
chiefly of the
vulgar.

Just as good morals,
if they are to be
maintained, have
need of the laws, so
the laws, if they are
to be observed, have
need of good morals.

For a long time
I have not said what I
believed, nor do I ever
believe what I say, and
if indeed sometimes I
do happen to tell the
truth, I hide it among
so many lies that it is
hard to find.

I assert once again as a truth to which history as a whole bears witness that men may second their fortune, but cannot oppose it; that they may weave its warp, but cannot break it. Yet they should never give up, because there is always hope, though they know not the end and more towards it along roads which cross one another and as yet are unexplored; and since there is hope, they should not despair, no matter what fortune brings or in what travail they find themselves.

Men are driven by two
principal impulses,
either by love
or by fear.

There is nothing
more important
than appearing
to be religious.

There is no other way
to guard yourself
against flattery
than by making men
understand that
telling you the truth
will not offend you.

The demands of a free
populace, too, are very
seldom harmful to liberty,
for they are due either to the
populace being oppressed or
to the suspicious that it is
going to be oppressed... and,
should these impressions be
false, a remedy is provided
in the public platform on
which some man of standing
can get up, appeal to the
crowd, and show that it is
mistaken. And though, as
Tully remarks, the populace
may be ignorant, it is
capable of grasping the truth
and readily yields when a
man, worthy of confidence,
lays the truth before it.

If a prince holds on
to his state by means
of mercenary armies,
he will never be
stable or secure.

Those who either from imprudence or want of sagacity avoid doing so, are always overwhelmed with servitude and poverty; for faithful servants are always servants, and honest men are always poor; nor do any ever escape from servitude but the bold and faithless, or from poverty, but the rapacious and fraudulent.

How laudable it is for
a prince to keep good
faith and live with
integrity, and not
with astuteness,
every one knows.
Still the experience
of our times shows
those princes to have
done great things
who have had little
regard for good faith,
and have been able by
astuteness to confuse
men's brains....

Whoever is the cause of another becoming powerful, is ruined himself; for that power is produced by him either through craft or force; and both of these are suspected by the one who has been raised to power.

It is better to act
and repent than
not to act
and regret.

One change always
leaves the way
open for the
establishment
of others.

When Scipio became
consul and was keen on
getting the province of
Africa, promising that
Carthage should be
completely destroyed,
and the senate would not
agree to this because
Fabius Maximus was
against it, he threatened
to appeal to the people,
for he knew full well how
pleasing such projects
are to the populace.

Men seldom rise from
low condition to high
rank without employing
either force or fraud,
unless that rank should
be attained either by
gift or inheritance.

It is the nature
of men to feel as
much obligated
for benefits
they confer
as for those
they receive.

A prince need
trouble little about
conspiracies when
the people are well
disposed, but when
they are hostile and
hold him in hatred,
then he must fear
everything and
everybody.

It should be borne in
mind that the temper
of the multitude is
fickle, and that
while it is easy to
persuade them of a
thing, it is hard to
fix them in that
persuasion.

Few men are brave
by nature, but good
discipline and
experience
make many so.

In order not to have to rob his subjects, to be able to defend himself, not to become poor and contemptible, and not to be forced to become rapacious, a prince must consider it of little importance if he incurs the reputation of being a miser, for this is one of the vices that permits him to rule.

I consider it a mark of
great prudence in a man
to abstain from threats
or any contemptuous
expressions, for neither
of these weaken the
enemy, but threats make
him more cautious, and
the other excites his
hatred, and a desire to
revenge himself.

We have not seen
great things done in
our time except by
those who have been
considered mean; the
rest have failed.

Where the
willingness is great,
the difficulties
cannot be great.

He who wishes
to be obeyed
must know
how to command.

The wise man should
always follow the
roads that have been
trodden by the great,
and imitate those who
have most excelled, so
that if he cannot reach
their perfection, he
may at least acquire
something of its
savour.

Wisdom consists
in being able to
distinguish
among dangers and
make a choice of
the least harmful.

It is not titles that
make men illustrious,
but men who make
titles illustrious.

Hatred is gained as
much by good works
as by evil.

The leader should
know how to enter
into evil when
necessity commands.

He who becomes a
Prince through the
favour of the people
should always keep on
good terms with them;
which it is easy for
him to do, since all
they ask is not to be
oppressed.

He who has once
begun to live by
rapine always finds
reasons for taking
what is not his.

There is no surer
sign of decay in a
country than to see
the rites of religion
held in contempt.

He who desires or attempts
to reform the government
of a state and wishes to
have it accepted, must at
least retain the semblance
of the old forms; so that it
may seem to the people that
there has been no change in
the institutions, even
though in fact they are
entirely different from
the old ones. For the great
majority of mankind
are satisfied with
appearances, as though
they were realities.

It is necessary for him
who lays out a state
and arranges laws for
it to presuppose that
all men are evil and
that they are always
going to act according
to the wickedness of
their spirits whenever
they have free scope.

A man should not
be injured and
then assigned
to important
administration
and control.

You know better than I
that in a Republic talent
is always suspect. A man
attains an elevated
position only when his
mediocrity prevents him
from being a threat to
others. And for this
reason a democracy is
never governed by the
most competent, but
rather by those whose
insignificance will not
jeopardize anyone else's
self-esteem.

They have not any
difficulties on the
way up because they
fly, but they have
many when they
reach the summit.

Men sooner forget the
death of their father
than the loss of their
patrimony.

The end of the
republic is to
enervate and to
weaken all other
bodies so as to
increase its
own body.

The first method
for estimating the
intelligence of a
ruler is to look at
the men he has
around him.

One can make this
generalization
about men: they are
ungrateful, fickle,
liars, and deceivers,
they shun danger and
are greedy for profit;
while you treat them
well, they are yours.
They would shed their
blood for you, risk
their property, their
lives, their children,
so long, as I said above,
as danger is remote; but
when you are in danger
they turn against you.

Men ought either to be
well treated or crushed,
because they can avenge
themselves of lighter
injuries, of more
serious ones they
cannot; therefore the
injury that is to be
done to a man ought to
be of such a kind that
one does not stand in
fear of revenge.

It is just as difficult
and dangerous to try
to free a people that
wants to remain
servile as it is to
enslave a people that
wants to remain free.

Whoever believes that
great advancement
and new benefits
make men forget old
injuries is mistaken.

You must know that
there are two methods
of fighting, the one by
law, the other by force:
the first method is
that of men, the second
of beasts; but as the
first method is often
insufficient, one must
have recourse to the
second. It is therefore
necessary to know well
how to use both the
beast and the man.

Wars begin when you
will, but they do not
end when you please.

A prince never lacks
legitimate reasons
to break his promise.

The people resemble a wild
beast, which, naturally
fierce and accustomed to
live in the woods, has been
brought up, as it were, in a
prison and in servitude,
and having by accident
got its liberty, not being
accustomed to search for
its food, and not knowing
where to conceal itself,
easily becomes the prey of
the first who seeks to
incarcerate it again.

Men walk almost
always in the paths
trodden by others,
proceeding in their
actions by imitation.

In all human affairs
one notices, if one
examines them
closely, that it is
impossible to remove
one inconvenience
without another
emerging.

The sinews of war
are not gold, but
good soldiers;
for gold alone will
not procure good
soldiers, but good
soldiers will always
procure gold.

And what physicians say about disease is applicable here: that at the beginning a disease is easy to cure but difficult to diagnose; but as time passes, not having been recognized or treated at the outset, it becomes easy to diagnose but difficult to cure. The same thing occurs in affairs of state; for by recognizing from afar the diseases that are spreading in the state (which is a gift given only to the prudent ruler), they can be cured quickly; but when, not having been recognized, they are not recognized and are left to grow to the extent that everyone recognizes them, there is no longer any cure.

So long as the great
majority of men are
not deprived of either
property or honour,
they are satisfied.

It has always been
the opinion and
judgment of wise men
that nothing can be
so uncertain as fame
or power not founded
on its own strength.

If you only notice
human proceedings,
you may observe that
all who attain great
power and riches, make
use of either force or
fraud; and what they
have acquired either
by deceit or violence,
in order to conceal the
disgraceful methods
of attainment, they
endeavor to sanctify
with the false title
of honest gains.

Men are so
imprudent that
they take up a diet
which, though it
tastes sweet, is
poisonous.

Any man who tries to
be good all the time is
bound to come to ruin
among the great
number who are not
good. Hence a prince
who wants to keep his
authority must learn
how not to be good, and
use that knowledge, or
refrain from using it,
as necessity requires.

Results are
often obtained by
impetuosity and
daring which
could never have
been obtained by
ordinary methods.

Men never do good
unless necessity
drives them to it;
but when they are
free to choose and
can do just as they
please, confusion
and disorder
become rampant.

There is nothing as
likely to succeed
as what the enemy
believes you
cannot attempt.

Men are so simple of
mind, and so much
dominated by their
immediate needs,
that a deceitful man
will always find
plenty who are
ready to be
deceived.

If malignity is hidden
for a time, it proceeds
from the unknown reason
that would not be known
because the experience
of the contrary had not
been seen, but time,
which is said to be the
father of every truth,
will cause it to be
discovered.

Whoever wishes to
foresee the future must
consult the past; for
human events ever
resemble those of
preceding times. This
arises from the fact that
they are produced by men
who ever have been, and
ever shall be, animated
by the same passions, and
thus they necessarily
have the same results.

Prudence consists
in knowing how to
distinguish degrees
of disadvantage, and
in accepting a less
evil as a good.

A wise prince will
seek means by which
his subjects will
always and in every
possible condition of
things have need of
his government, and
then they will always
be faithful to him.

The promise given
was a necessity
of the past:
the word broken
is a necessity
of the present.

I am firmly convinced, therefore, that to set up a republic which is to last a long time, the way to set about it is to constitute it as Sparta and Venice were constituted; to place it in a strong position, and so to fortify it that no one will dream of taking it by a sudden assault; and, on the other hand, not to make it so large as to appear formidable to its neighbors. It should in this way be able to enjoy its form of government for a long time. For war is made on a commonwealth for two reasons: to subjugate it, and for fear of being subjugated by it.

A prince should make himself feared in such a way that if he does not gain love, he at any rate avoids hatred; for fear and the absence of hatred may well go together, and will be always attained by one who abstains from interfering with the property of his citizens and subjects or with their women.

A wise ruler should
rely on what is under
his own control, not
on what is under the
control of others.

Since a prince is
necessitated to play the
animal well, he chooses
among the beasts the fox
and the lion, because the
lion does not protect
himself from traps; the
fox does not protect
himself from wolves.
The prince must be a fox,
therefore, to recognize
the traps and a lion to
frighten the wolves.

And in examining their life and deeds it will be seen that they owed nothing to fortune but the opportunity which gave them matter to be shaped into the form that they thought fit; and without that opportunity their powers would have been wasted, and without their powers the opportunity would have come in vain.

A prudent ruler ought
not to keep faith when
by so doing it would be
against his interest, and
when the reasons which
made him bind himself no
longer exist. If men were
all good, this precept
would not be a good one;
but as they are bad, and
would not observe their
faith with you, so you
are not bound to keep
faith with them.

War is just which is
necessary, and arms
are hallowed when
there is no other
hope but in them.

States that rise quickly, just as all the other things of nature that are born and grow rapidly, cannot have roots and ramifications; the first bad weather kills them.

God is not willing
to do everything,
and thus take away
our free will and
that share of glory
which belongs to us.